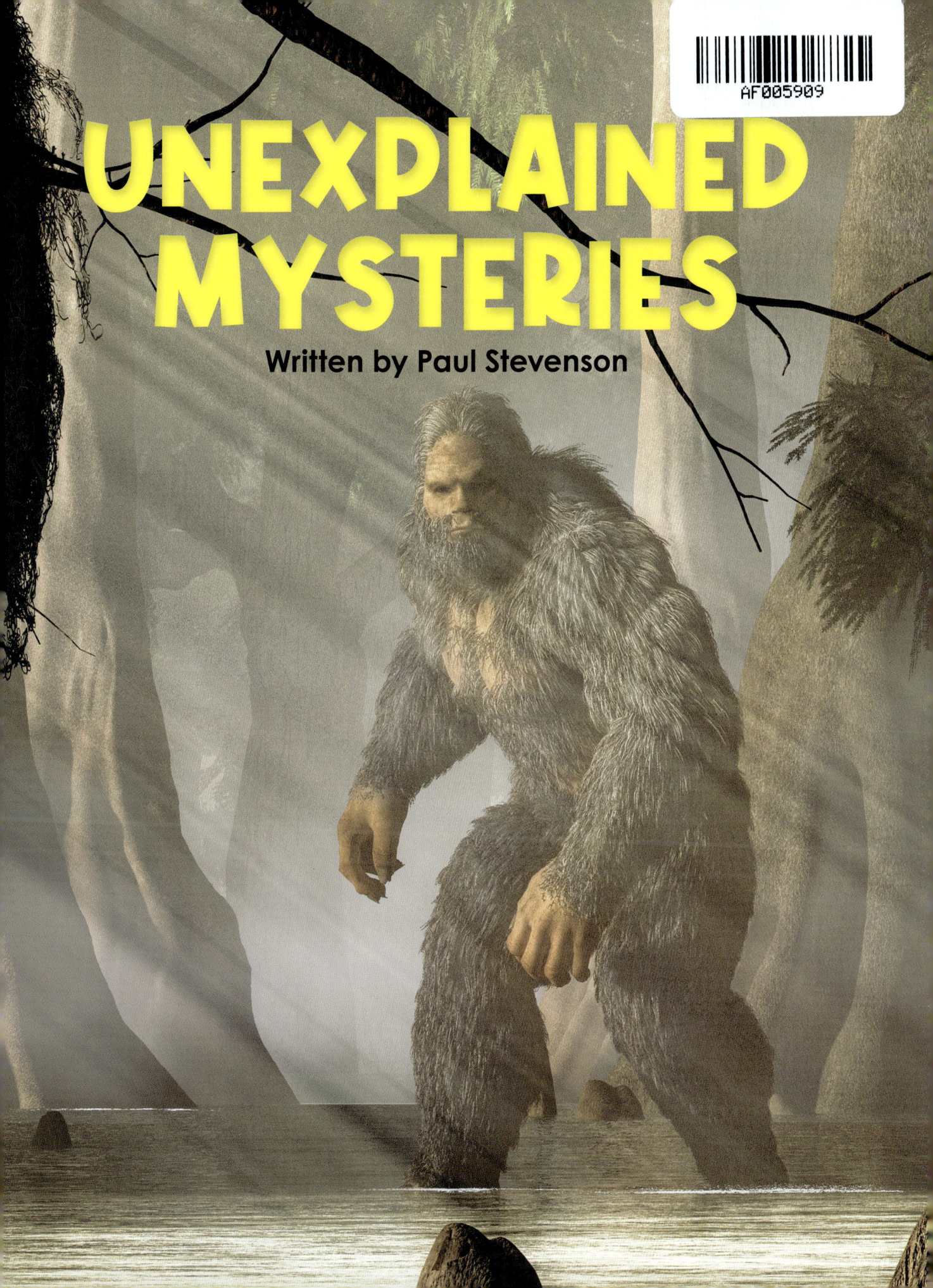

UNEXPLAINED MYSTERIES

Written by Paul Stevenson

CONTENTS

Mysterious Beasts	4
Loch Ness Monster	6
Mountain Beast	8
Bigfoot	10
Killer Kraken	12
Sea Monsters?	14
Mongolian Death Worm	16
Dragons in the Skies	18
Prehistoric Beasts	20
Night Killer	22
Mythical Mermaids	24
Prowling Werewolves	26
A World of Mystery	28
Cryptozoology	30
Glossary	31
Index	32

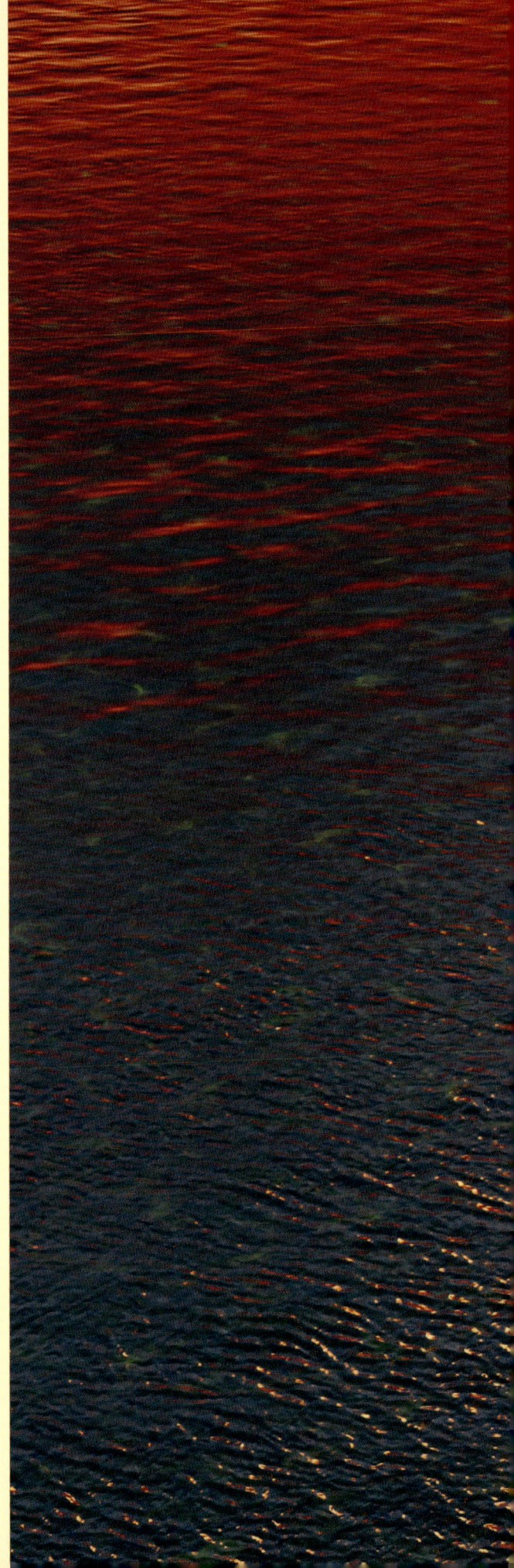

First published in 2024 by
Hungry Tomato Ltd
F15, Old Bakery Studios,
Blewetts Wharf, Malpas Road,
Truro, Cornwall,
TR1 1QH, UK.

Thanks to our editor, Julie Tofflemire.

Copyright © 2024 Hungry Tomato Ltd

No part of this publication may be reproduced, stored in a retrieval system, or transmitted in any form or by any means, electronic, mechanical, photocopying, recording, or otherwise, without prior written permission of the copyright owner.

A CIP catalogue record for this book is available from the British Library.

ISBN 9781835691168
Printed in China

Discover more at
www.hungrytomato.com

Neither the publisher nor the author shall be liable for any bodily harm or damage to property whatsoever that may caused as a result of conducting any of the activites in this book.

All words in **BOLD** can be found in the glossary.

DISCLAIMER:
These are only stories and tales. Read about and look at the evidence to decide if you believe in each mystery or not. Never go exploring on your own.

MYSTERIOUS BEASTS

We don't know everything about our world. There are still some mysteries that can't be explained!

When night falls, what can be found deep in the **wilderness**?

What **lurks** under the ocean's surface?

Can we trust the reports of mysterious encounters?
Or are these just made-up stories?

You never know what may be hiding nearby...watching.

IT'S TIME TO TAKE A CLOSER LOOK...

LOCH NESS MONSTER

For nearly 1,500 years, people have told stories of a secret beast in Scotland, United Kingdom. They say it lives in a deep lake called Loch Ness.

In 1930, three young men were fishing on Loch Ness. Suddenly, a large creature swam towards their boat.

The creature turned away about 300 metres from the boat. The fishermen were sure it was the Loch Ness Monster.

In 1934, a photo of the monster was published in a London newspaper. The photo became famous, but it turned out to be a **hoax**. The monster was just a model!

Does Loch Ness hide a secret beast?

MOUNTAIN BEAST

For centuries, the people who live in the mountains of Tibet and Nepal have talked of the Yeti. They say that...

It is over 2 metres tall.

The Yeti has thick, dark hair.

It walks like a human.

It also smells very bad!

In 2003, a girl in Nepal said she saw the Yeti.

The girl was looking after her yaks. She said the animals were attacked by the Yeti.

The Yeti was so strong it was able to rip the skin off the yaks. It even tore the legs off one yak.

The girl thought she was next. However, the beast disappeared back into the forest.

Yak

BIGFOOT

In the wild places of North America, there are stories of a beast called Bigfoot.

In 1967, a man named Roger Patterson filmed a Bigfoot in the northwest of America. The beast was at least 2 metres tall.

It walked off towards some woods. Then it turned and looked towards Patterson.

Some scientists say the film shows an unknown animal. Others say it is just a man in an ape suit!

Does Bigfoot really exist?

KILLER KRAKEN

For hundreds of years, sailors told stories of a giant sea monster called the Kraken.

It was described as a squid-like creature that could destroy ships. The Kraken would first attack the ship with its powerful **tentacles**.

If that didn't work, it would swim quickly round and round the ship. This would create a **whirlpool** to pull the ship underwater.

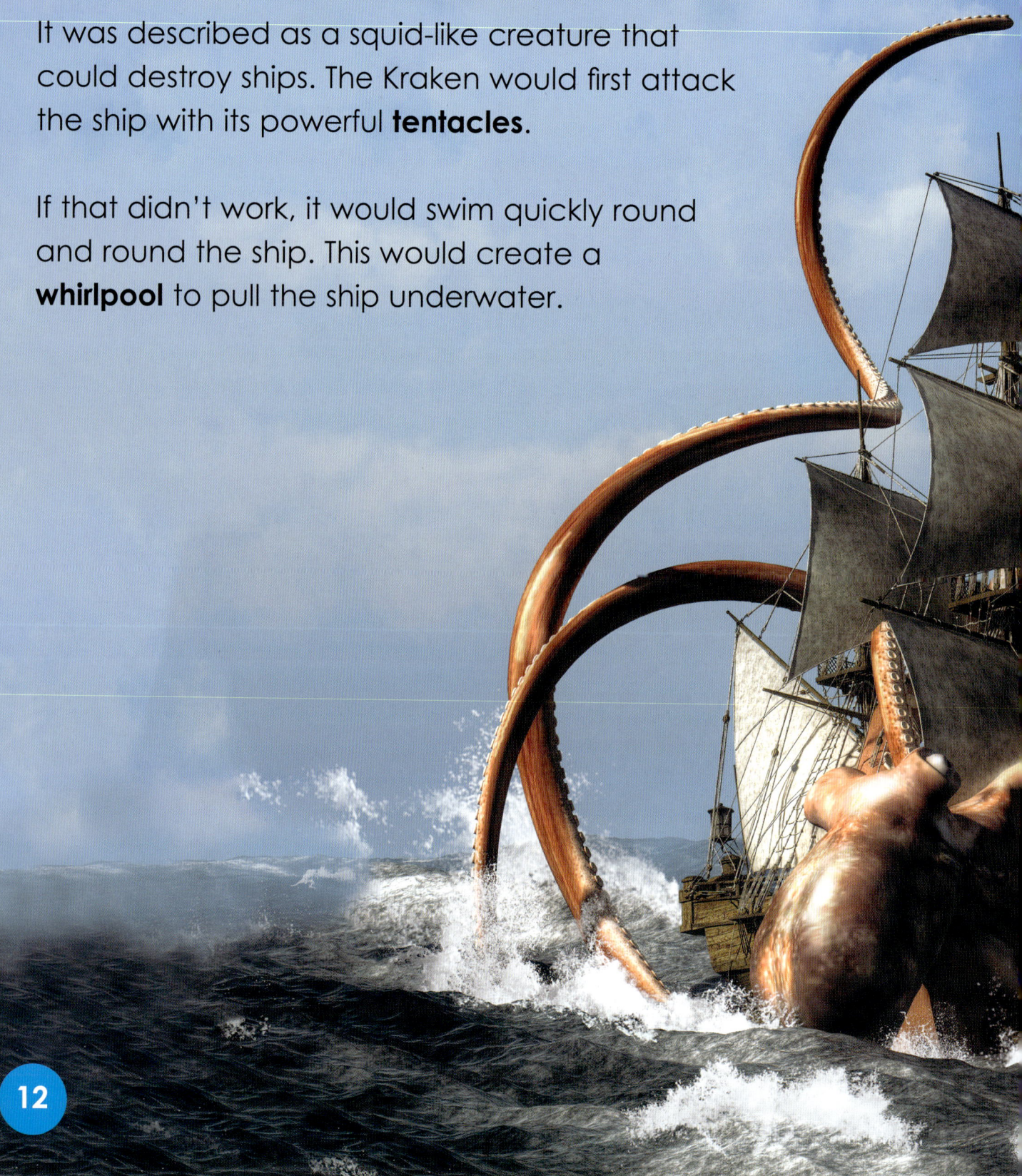

SEA MONSTERS?

Could there be giant, monster-like creatures living in the ocean?

Perhaps the Kraken was actually a giant squid.
Giant squid live deep under the sea.

The largest giant squid recorded so far was about 13 metres in length!

Tentacles

Suckers

A giant squid could cling to a boat with the suckers on its tentacles.

Perhaps some sea monsters were actually oarfish.

These creatures are usually about 3 metres long. But the longest oarfish found was an incredible 11 metres long!

Oarfish skeleton

MONGOLIAN DEATH WORM

Among the vast sands of the Gobi Desert, there is something that strikes fear into the hearts of many – the Mongolian Death Worm.

Some say the dreaded creature is just a part of **folklore**, but others are convinced that it is real. It is said to be 0.6–1.5 metres long and look like a worm with a thick body.

Mongolian Death Worm

The Mongolian Death Worm attacks its victims and then burrows underground. It is said to have **poisonous saliva** that acts quickly.

Some say the Mongolian Death Worm can kill its victims with electric shocks!

Though its existence has not been proven, lots of reports and **rumours** continue to spread.

DRAGONS IN THE SKIES

Myths about dragons have been around for thousands of years. Some people claim to have seen dragons. But are these reports fact or fiction?

In the early 1800s, a reporter interviewed elderly people who lived in Wales, United Kingdom.

Many of them said they had seen winged serpents as children. The beasts had feathery wings and skin that sparkled like jewels.

In 2001, a group of scientists were working in eastern Wales. They claimed to have seen a green beast flying in the air.

It seems you can see a lot of dragons in Wales, even on its flag!

PREHISTORIC BEASTS

In prehistoric times, flying reptiles called pterosaurs ruled the skies. People in Texas, USA, have repeatedly reported seeing these same beasts.

In 1976, two schoolteachers in San Antonio saw a pair of flying creatures with **wingspans** of 4.5–6 metres.

That same year, a man near Harlington went outside to investigate a noise and found himself face to face with a 1.2 metre bird-like creature with enormous eyes.

In 1982, an ambulance technician saw a pterosaur-like beast swoop down over the road while driving in southern Texas.

In 2013, two more reports came in of something large and dark flying over San Antonio.

Could prehistoric pterosaurs still exist today?

NIGHT KILLER

In parts of North and South America, people say chupacabras suck animals' blood and then leave them for dead.

Chupacabras are known to be fierce, though they are not much bigger than an average dog. Their eyes glow red, and they have deadly **fangs**.

In the late 1980s and early 1990s, farmers in Puerto Rico started reporting more and more chupacabra sightings.

People say chupacabras attack goats, sheep and chickens at night.

MYTHICAL MERMAIDS

Although stories of mermaid sightings date back as far as 1000 BCE, there are still reports of these water characters.

During a **reservoir**-building project in Zimbabwe in 2012, workers reported being disturbed by mermaids! The crew was terrified and refused to return to work.

Replacement workers were brought in, but they also said they spotted the mermaids.

SOME PEOPLE BELIEVE THAT MANATEES ARE OFTEN MISTAKEN FOR MERMAIDS.

Manatee

PROWLING WEREWOLVES

Staffordshire in England may be a hotspot for modern-day werewolves! One report shows twenty sightings in the area of Cannock Chase.

A survey from 1975 included people claiming to have seen a snarling beast. It raised itself onto its back legs before escaping into the woods.

Full moon

In 2007, several people contacted the West Midlands Ghost Club to report a creature that looked like a werewolf.

They said it was nearly 2.1 metres tall when it stood up. No one was able to record it before it ran away.

One **paranormal** expert thought these beasts might have been living in nearby mines.

A WORLD OF MYSTERY

Stories of mysterious beasts have been told around the world for hundreds of years. Could some of these beasts really be out there?

GIANT APE-MEN

Native Americans call Bigfoot "Sasquatch". This means "wild man".

MOUNTAIN BEASTS

Yeti means "beast of the mountains".

SEA MONSTERS

Giant squid can have eyes as big as dinner plates.

STRANGE SWIMMERS

Mermaids are thought to protect their waters.

LAKE MONSTERS

The Loch Ness Monster is known as "Nessie".

FLYING CREATURES

The pterosaur had a body as tall as a giraffe.

Perhaps there are even more beasts we haven't encountered yet. Keep watching. They may be closer than you think...

CRYPTOZOOLOGY

Cryptozoology is the study of mysterious creatures.

It is considered a **pseudoscience**, which means it does not follow the **scientific method**. Cryptozoology focuses on creatures whose existence is uncertain.

WHAT DO CRYPTOZOOLOGISTS DO?

- Collect data about possible sightings
- Interview **eyewitnesses** and determine how **trustworthy** they are
- Try to gather physical proof of a creature's presence

ARE YOU BRAVE ENOUGH TO HAVE A MYSTERIOUS ENCOUNTER OF YOUR OWN?

GLOSSARY

eyewitnesses – people who saw something happen.

fangs – long, sharp teeth.

folklore – the traditional stories and customs of a group of people.

hoax – a practical joke.

hotspot – a place where a lot of a certain activity is happening.

lurk – to hide and wait secretly, especially to do something bad.

paranormal – not able to be explained by science.

poisonous – causing illness or death if taken into the body.

pseudoscience – an idea that seems like science but isn't.

reptiles – cold-blooded animals with backbones. Snakes, lizards, turtles and crocodiles are all reptiles.

reservoir – an artificial lake where water is stored for human use.

rumours – stories or information that people talk about that may or may not be true.

saliva – the liquid in your mouth that is used to break down food.

scientific method – a way to establish facts through testing and experiments.

tentacle – a long body part that is used for touching and holding things.

trustworthy – honest and dependable. A trustworthy person tells the truth.

whirlpool – a place in water where the currents move round and round quickly.

wilderness – an area in which few people live that is still in its natural state.

wingspan – the measurement of a bird's or plane's wings from wing tip to wing tip.

INDEX

A
attacks 9, 12 17, 22

B
Bigfoot 10-11, 28
birds 20

C
chupacabra 22-23
cryptozoology 30

D
dragons 18-19

E
England 26

G
giant squid 14-15, 29
Gobi desert 16

K
Kraken 12-13, 14

L
Loch Ness Monster 6-7, 29

M
manatees 25
mermaids 24-25, 29
Mongolian Death Worm 16-17

N
Nepal 8-9
North America 10-11, 22

O
oarfish 15

P
Patterson, Roger 10
pterosaurs 20-21, 29
Puerto Rico 22

S
Scotland 6-7
sea monsters 12-13, 14-15, 29

South America 20
squid, giant 14-15, 29

T
tentacles 12, 14-15, 31
Tibet 8

U
United Kingdom 6-7, 18, 26-27
USA 20-21

W
Wales 18
werewolves 26-27
wings 18-19, 20-21, 31

Y
yaks 9
Yeti 8-9, 28

Z
Zimbabwe 24

Picture credits:
(t=top; b=bottom; m=middle; l=left; r=right):
Shutterstock: Adansijav Official 2-3bg, 29mr; Alex Coan 13tl; Andrea Izzotti 22bl; Andreiuc88 30m; Andreiuc88 4b; Andrey_Kuzmin 5bl; Artem Avetisyan 22-23bg; Bilanol 18-19bg; Computer earth 19bg; Daniel Eskridge 1bg, 10-11bg, 21bg, 29bl, 31b; Denis—S 26b; Don Fink 6-7bg; Evgeniia Demi 29ml; ForeverLee 24-25bg; GSoul 27b; Janis Petranis 20b; JM-MEDIA 28ml; Jose L Vilchez 14-15bg; Lokman Hamid 13b; Lubomira08 7ml; Mikeldray 12b; Paul Juser 25tl; RikoBest 8bg; Rob Atherton 5t; Rui Palma 29tr; Runa0410 16-17bg; Sicegame 14ml; Warpaint 28mr.

Every effort has been made to trace the copyright holders, and we apologise in advance for any unintentional omissions. We would be pleased to insert the appropriate acknowledgements in any subsequent edition of this publication.